This book belongs to an awesome gymnast called:

Year:

Remember, everything you need to be great is already inside you

Table of Contents

About Me

Year _____   Age _____   Level _____

Club _____

Favorite Apparatus: _____

Best Apparatus: _____

Favorite move: _____

Strengths:

Hard Worker ☐   Speed ☐   Strength ☐   Team Player

Listening ☐   Persistence ☐   Flexibility ☐   Practice

Other ☐   _____

Goals for the Year

_____
_____
_____
_____

I promise to improve on:

_____
_____
_____

Notes _____

_____

_____

I love my club because

_____

_____

Favorite famous gymnast _____

Favorite coach _____

My Gymnastics Friends _____

_____

Funniest _____

Chattiest _____

Bravest _____

This is my favorite leotard

Color

_____

Design

_____

Class Schedule

Safety Tip Sheet

- Always warm up and stretch before doing gymnastics.

- Only practice on padded floors, never on a hard surface.

- Mats should be placed under the equipment and properly secured at all times.

- Have a coach spotting for all new or difficult skills.

- Let the coach know if you are uncomfortable with a gymnastic move. If the coach isn't supportive, tell a parent or an administrator.

- Never try a stunt at a game or competition that you haven't practiced many times.

- Follow gym rules for your club such as:
  - 1 person on a trampoline at a time
  - when jumping into a foam pit, land on feet, bottom, or back;
  - no diving headfirst or landing on the knees
  - 1 person at a time on the equipment (such as uneven bars, rings, or balance beam)
  - No training alone
  - Wear gymnastic clothes that won't get caught on any of the equipment.
  - No jewelry
  - No gum chewing

- Stop training if you get hurt or feel pain. See a medical professional if injury persists over training sessions.

- Play different sports throughout the year to prevent overuse injuries.

- Know the team plan for emergencies.
  This includes calling 911 for a head, neck, or back injury and NOT moving the hurt gymnast.

GOAL TRACKER

Goal: _____

_____

Action Steps: _____

1. _____

2. _____

3. _____

By Date: _____

Goal: _____

_____

Action Steps: _____

1. _____

2. _____

3. _____

By Date: _____

Goal: _____

_____

Action Steps: _____

1. _____

2. _____

3. _____

By Date: _____

Goal: _____

_____

Action Steps: _____

1. _____

2. _____

3. _____

By Date: _____

Progress Notes: _____

_____

_____

_____

_____

Week ···········

*Your limitation—
it's only your imagination.*

Monday

_____

Tuesday

_____

Wednesday

_____

Thursday

_____

Friday

_____

Saturday

_____

Sunday

_____

Priorities

To Do

- ★
- ★
- ★
- ★

Notes

My Training Week

Coach Name: _____

Hours Trained: _____

Achievements: _____

How I felt ☹ 😐 😐 ☺ 😃

Conditioning notes

Skill:	Rep:

Coach Said:

Best thing this week:

I am
grateful for

Week ....

Sometimes later becomes never. Do it Now.

Monday

_____

Tuesday

_____

Wednesday

_____

Thursday

_____

Friday

_____

Saturday

_____

Sunday

_____

Priorities

To Do

★

★

★

★

Notes

My Training Week

Coach Name: _____

Hours Trained: _____

Achievements: _____

How I felt ☹ 😕 😐 🙂 😃

Conditioning notes

Skill:	Rep:

Coach Said:

Best thing this Week:

I am grateful for

Week ....

> *Great things never come from comfort zones.*

Monday

_____

Tuesday

_____

Wednesday

_____

Thursday

_____

Friday

_____

Saturday

_____

Sunday

_____

Priorities

To Do

- ★
- ★
- ★
- ★

Notes

My Training Week

Coach Name: _____

Hours Trained: _____

Achievements: _____

How I felt ☹ 😐 😑 🙂 😄

Conditioning notes

Skill:	Rep:

Coach Said:

Best thing this week:

I am grateful for

Dream it. Wish it. Do it.

Week ....

Monday

_____

Tuesday

_____

Wednesday

_____

Thursday

_____

Friday

_____

Saturday

_____

Sunday

_____

Priorities

To Do

- ★
- ★
- ★
- ★

Notes

My Training Week

Coach Name: _____

Hours Trained: _____

Achievements: _____

How I felt   ☹   😐   😐   🙂   😃

Conditioning notes

Skill:	Rep:

Coach Said:

Best thing this Week:

I am grateful for

Week ....

Success doesn't just find you. You have to go out & get it.

Monday
_____

Tuesday
_____

Wednesday
_____

Thursday
_____

Friday
_____

Saturday
_____

Sunday
_____

Priorities

To Do
- ★
- ★
- ★
- ★

Notes

My Training Week

Coach Name: _____

Hours Trained: _____

Achievements: _____

How I felt ☹ 🙂 😐 🙂 😃

Conditioning notes

Skill:	Rep:

Coach Said:

Best thing this Week:

I am
grateful for

Week ....

Dream bigger. Do bigger.

Monday

_____

Tuesday

_____

Wednesday

_____

Thursday

_____

Friday

_____

Saturday

_____

Sunday

_____

Priorities

To Do

- ★
- ★
- ★
- ★

Notes

My Training Week

Coach Name: _____

Hours Trained: _____

Achievements: _____

How I felt ☹ 😕 😐 🙂 😄

Conditioning notes

Skill:	Rep:

Coach Said:

Best thing this week:

I am grateful for

Week ....

Don't stop when you are tired, Stop when you are done.

Monday

_____

Tuesday

_____

Wednesday

_____

Thursday

_____

Friday

_____

Saturday

_____

Sunday

_____

Priorities

To Do

- ★
- ★
- ★
- ★

Notes

My Training Week

Coach Name: _____

Hours Trained: _____

Achievements: _____

How I felt ☹ 😐 😐 ☺ 😄

Conditioning notes

Skill:	Rep:

Coach Said:

Best thing this Week:

I am grateful for

Week ....

Wake up with determination. Go to bed with satisfaction.

Monday

_____

Tuesday

_____

Wednesday

_____

Thursday

_____

Friday

_____

Saturday

_____

Sunday

_____

Priorities

To Do
- ★
- ★
- ★
- ★

Notes

My Training Week

Coach Name: _____

Hours Trained: _____

Achievements: _____

How I felt ☹ 😐 😑 ☺ 😃

Conditioning notes

Skill:	Rep:

Coach Said:

Best thing this Week:

I am grateful for

Week ◆◆◆◆◆◆◆◆

Do something today that your future self will thank you for.

	Priorities
Monday	
_____	
Tuesday	
_____	
Wednesday	**To Do**
_____	★
Thursday	★
_____	★
Friday	★
_____	
Saturday	**Notes**
_____	
Sunday	
_____	

My Training Week

Coach Name: _____

Hours Trained: _____

Achievements: _____

How I felt ☹ 🙂 😐 🙂 😃

Conditioning notes

Skill:	Rep:

Coach Said:

Best thing this week:

I am
grateful for

Little things make big days.

Week ◆◆◆◆◆◆

Monday

_____

Tuesday

_____

Wednesday

_____

Thursday

_____

Friday

_____

Saturday

_____

Sunday

_____

Priorities

To Do

- ★
- ★
- ★
- ★

Notes

My Training Week

Coach Name: _____

Hours Trained: _____

Achievements: _____

How I felt ☹ 😕 😐 🙂 😃

Conditioning notes

Skill:	Rep:

Coach Said:

Best thing this week:

I am grateful for

Week ●◆◆◆◆◆◆◆◆◆

It's going to be hard – but hard doesn't mean impossible.

Monday

_____

Tuesday

_____

Wednesday

_____

Thursday

_____

Friday

_____

Saturday

_____

Sunday

_____

Priorities

To Do

★

★

★

★

Notes

◆◆◆◆◆◆◆◆◆◆◆◆◆◆◆◆

My Training Week

Coach Name: _____

Hours Trained: _____

Achievements: _____

How I felt ☹ 😕 😐 🙂 😄

Conditioning notes

Skill:	Rep:

Coach Said:

Best thing this Week:

I am
grateful for

Week ....

Don't wait for opportunity – create it.

Monday

_____

Tuesday

_____

Wednesday

_____

Thursday

_____

Friday

_____

Saturday

_____

Sunday

_____

Priorities

To Do

* ★
* ★
* ★
* ★

Notes

My Training Week

Coach Name: _____

Hours Trained: _____

Achievements: _____

How I felt ☹ ☺ 😐 🙂 😃

Conditioning notes

Skill:	Rep:

Coach Said:

Best thing this week:

I am grateful for

Week •••••••••

Monday

_____

Tuesday

_____

Wednesday

_____

Thursday

_____

Friday

_____

Saturday

_____

Sunday

_____

Priorities

To Do

*
*
*
*

Notes

My Training Week

Coach Name: _____

Hours Trained: _____

Achievements: _____

How I felt   ☹ 😐 😐 🙂 😃

Conditioning notes

Skill:	Rep:

Coach Said: Best thing this week:

I am grateful for

Week .... •◆•◆•◆•◆•◆

The key to success is to focus on goals, not obstacles.

Monday

_____

Tuesday

_____

Wednesday

_____

Thursday

_____

Friday

_____

Saturday

_____

Sunday

_____

Priorities

To Do

- ★
- ★
- ★
- ★

Notes

My Training Week

Coach Name: _____

Hours Trained: _____

Achievements: _____

How I felt ☹ 😐 😐 🙂 😄

Conditioning notes

Skill:	Rep:

Coach Said:

Best thing this week:

I am
grateful for

Week ....

Monday

_____

Tuesday

_____

Wednesday

_____

Thursday

_____

Friday

_____

Saturday

_____

Sunday

_____

Dream it. Believe it.
Build it.

Priorities

To Do

*
*
*
*

Notes

My Training Week

Coach Name: _____

Hours Trained: _____

Achievements: _____

How I felt   ☹ 🙁 😐 🙂 😄

Conditioning notes

Skill:	Rep:

Coach Said:

Best thing this week:

I am grateful for

Week ◆◆◆◆◆◆◆◆

You've come so far – don't quit now.

Monday
_____

Tuesday
_____

Wednesday
_____

Thursday
_____

Friday
_____

Saturday
_____

Sunday
_____

Priorities

To Do
★
★
★
★

Notes

My Training Week

Coach Name: _____

Hours Trained: _____

Achievements: _____

How I felt ☹ 😐 😐 🙂 😃

Conditioning notes

Skill:	Rep:

Coach Said:

Best thing this week:

I am grateful for

Week ....

To reach your goals, you must grab on with both hands.

Monday

_____

Tuesday

_____

Wednesday

_____

Thursday

_____

Friday

_____

Saturday

_____

Sunday

_____

Priorities

To Do

★

★

★

★

Notes

My Training Week

Coach Name: _____

Hours Trained: _____

Achievements: _____

How I felt ☹ 😕 😐 🙂 😃

Conditioning notes

Skill:	Rep:

Coach Said:

Best thing this week:

I am grateful for

You are your only limit.

Week ....

Monday

_____

Tuesday

_____

Wednesday

_____

Thursday

_____

Friday

_____

Saturday

_____

Sunday

_____

Priorities

To Do

- ★
- ★
- ★
- ★

Notes

My Training Week

Coach Name: _____

Hours Trained: _____

Achievements: _____

How I felt ☹ 😕 😐 🙂 😄

Conditioning notes

Skill:	Rep:

Coach Said:

Best thing this week:

I am grateful for

Play like you are in first.
Train like you are in second.

Week ....

Monday

_____

Tuesday

_____

Wednesday

_____

Thursday

_____

Friday

_____

Saturday

_____

Sunday

_____

Priorities

To Do
- ★
- ★
- ★
- ★

Notes

My Training Week

Coach Name: _____

Hours Trained: _____

Achievements: _____

How I felt ☹ 😕 😐 🙂 😃

Conditioning notes

Skill:	Rep:

Coach Said:

Best thing this week:

I am
grateful for

I can and I will.

Week ....

Monday
_____

Tuesday
_____

Wednesday
_____

Thursday
_____

Friday
_____

Saturday
_____

Sunday
_____

Priorities

To Do
- ★
- ★
- ★
- ★

Notes

My Training Week

Coach Name: _____

Hours Trained: _____

Achievements: _____

How I felt ☹ 😕 😐 🙂 😃

Conditioning notes

Skill:	Rep:

Coach Said:

Best thing this week:

I am grateful for

Week ....

Monday

_____

Tuesday

_____

Wednesday

_____

Thursday

_____

Friday

_____

Saturday

_____

Sunday

_____

Priorities

To Do

- ★
- ★
- ★
- ★

Notes

My Training Week

Coach Name: _____

Hours Trained: _____

Achievements: _____

How I felt ☹ 🙂 😐 🙂 😄

Conditioning notes

Skill:	Rep:

Coach Said:

Best thing this week:

I am
grateful for

Week ••••••••

*Pain is temporary -
Greatness is forever.*

Monday

_____

Tuesday

_____

Wednesday

_____

Thursday

_____

Friday

_____

Saturday

_____

Sunday

_____

Priorities

To Do

★

★

★

★

Notes

My Training Week

Coach Name: _____

Hours Trained: _____

Achievements: _____

How I felt ☹ 😕 😐 🙂 😃

Conditioning notes

Skill:	Rep:

Coach Said:

Best thing this week:

I am grateful for

You are stronger than you think.

Week ··········

Monday

_____

Tuesday

_____

Wednesday

_____

Thursday

_____

Friday

_____

Saturday

_____

Sunday

_____

Priorities

To Do

- ★
- ★
- ★
- ★

Notes

My Training Week

Coach Name: _____

Hours Trained: _____

Achievements: _____

How I felt   ☹ 😕 😐 🙂 😄

Conditioning notes

Skill:	Rep:

Coach Said:

Best thing this week:

I am grateful for

Week ◆◆◆◆◆◆◆◆◆

If you don't leap you will never know what its like to fly.

Monday

_____

Tuesday

_____

Wednesday

_____

Thursday

_____

Friday

_____

Saturday

_____

Sunday

_____

Priorities

To Do

★
★
★
★

Notes

My Training Week

Coach Name: _____

Hours Trained: _____

Achievements: _____

How I felt ☹ ☺ 😐 🙂 😄

Conditioning notes

Skill:	Rep:

Coach Said:

Best thing this week:

I am grateful for

Week ◆◆◆◆◆◆◆

Monday

_____

Tuesday

_____

Wednesday

_____

Thursday

_____

Friday

_____

Saturday

_____

Sunday

_____

Priorities

To Do
- ★
- ★
- ★
- ★

Notes

My Training Week

Coach Name: _____

Hours Trained: _____

Achievements: _____

How I felt   ☹ ☺ ☻ ☺ ☺

Conditioning notes

Skill:	Rep:

Coach Said:

Best thing this week:

I am grateful for

Week ◆◆◆◆◆◆◆

Monday
_____

Tuesday
_____

Wednesday
_____

Thursday
_____

Friday
_____

Saturday
_____

Sunday
_____

Priorities

To Do

- ★
- ★
- ★
- ★

Notes

My Training Week

Coach Name: _____

Hours Trained: _____

Achievements: _____

How I felt 😦 🙂 😐 🙂 😁

Conditioning notes

Skill:	Rep:

Coach Said:

Best thing this week:

I am grateful for

Week ━━━━━━━━

Losers quit when they are tired. Winners quit when they have won.

Monday

_____

Tuesday

_____

Wednesday

_____

Thursday

_____

Friday

_____

Saturday

_____

Sunday

_____

Priorities

To Do

- ★
- ★
- ★
- ★

Notes

My Training Week

Coach Name: _____

Hours Trained: _____

Achievements: _____

How I felt ☹ 🙂 😐 🙂 😃

Conditioning notes

Skill:	Rep:

Coach Said:

Best thing this week:

I am grateful for

Take your dreams seriously.

Week ....

Monday

_____

Tuesday

_____

Wednesday

_____

Thursday

_____

Friday

_____

Saturday

_____

Sunday

_____

Priorities

To Do

★

★

★

★

Notes

My Training Week

Coach Name: _____

Hours Trained: _____

Achievements: _____

How I felt (☹) (😕) (😐) (🙂) (😃)

Conditioning notes

Skill:	Rep:

Coach Said:

Best thing this week:

I am
grateful for

Week ●◆◆◆◆◆◆◆◆

Forget the mistake - remember the lesson.

Monday

_____

Tuesday

_____

Wednesday

_____

Thursday

_____

Friday

_____

Saturday

_____

Sunday

_____

Priorities

To Do

★

★

★

★

Notes

My Training Week

Coach Name: _____

Hours Trained: _____

Achievements: _____

How I felt ☹ 🙂 😐 🙂 😄

Conditioning notes

Skill:	Rep:

Coach Said:

Best thing this Week:

I am grateful for

Week ●◆◆◆◆◆◆◆◆►

Work hard – dream big.

Monday

_____

Tuesday

_____

Wednesday

_____

Thursday

_____

Friday

_____

Saturday

_____

Sunday

_____

Priorities

To Do

- ★
- ★
- ★
- ★

Notes

My Training Week

Coach Name: _____

Hours Trained: _____

Achievements: _____

How I felt 😦 🙂 😐 🙂 😃

Conditioning notes

Skill:	Rep:

Coach Said:

Best thing this Week:

I am grateful for

Week ••••••••

Make it happen – Shock everyone.

Monday

_____

Tuesday

_____

Wednesday

_____

Thursday

_____

Friday

_____

Saturday

_____

Sunday

_____

Priorities

To Do

* ★
* ★
* ★
* ★

Notes

My Training Week

Coach Name: _____

Hours Trained: _____

Achievements: _____

How I felt ☹ 🙁 😐 🙂 😃

Conditioning notes

Skill:	Rep:

Coach Said:

Best thing this week:

I am grateful for

Week ....

Monday

_____

Tuesday

_____

Wednesday

_____

Thursday

_____

Friday

_____

Saturday

_____

Sunday

_____

Priorities

To Do

- ★
- ★
- ★
- ★

Notes

My Training Week

Coach Name: _____

Hours Trained: _____

Achievements: _____

How I felt ☹ 😕 😐 🙂 😄

Conditioning notes

Skill:	Rep:

Coach Said:

Best thing this Week:

I am grateful for

Work Hard, Hussle, Grind.

Week ....

Monday

_____

Tuesday

_____

Wednesday

_____

Thursday

_____

Friday

_____

Saturday

_____

Sunday

_____

Priorities

To Do

★

★

★

★

Notes

My Training Week

Coach Name: _____

Hours Trained: _____

Achievements: _____

How I felt ☹ 😐 😐 🙂 😀

Conditioning notes

Skill:	Rep:

Coach Said:

Best thing this week:

I am grateful for

Week ....

Be driven.

Monday

_____

Tuesday

_____

Wednesday

_____

Thursday

_____

Friday

_____

Saturday

_____

Sunday

_____

Priorities

To Do

★

★

★

★

Notes

My Training Week

Coach Name: _____

Hours Trained: _____

Achievements: _____

How I felt ☹ 🙂 😐 ☺ 😃

Conditioning notes

Skill:	Rep:

Coach Said:

Best thing this week:

I am grateful for

Be hungry.

Week ━━━━━━━━▶

Monday
_____

Tuesday
_____

Wednesday
_____

Thursday
_____

Friday
_____

Saturday
_____

Sunday
_____

Priorities

To Do
★
★
★
★

Notes

My Training Week

Coach Name: _____

Hours Trained: _____

Achievements: _____

How I felt ☹ 🙂 😐 🙂 😄

Conditioning notes

Skill:	Rep:

Coach Said:

Best thing this Week:

I am grateful for

Be positive.

Week ....

Monday
_____

Tuesday
_____

Wednesday
_____

Thursday
_____

Friday
_____

Saturday
_____

Sunday
_____

Priorities

To Do
★
★
★
★

Notes

My Training Week

Coach Name: _____

Hours Trained: _____

Achievements: _____

How I felt   ☹ 🙂 😐 🙂 😄

Conditioning notes

Skill:	Rep:

Coach Said:

Best thing this week:

I am grateful for

Week ◆◆◆◆◆◆◆

It's not about how good you are,
but how bad you want it.

Monday

_____

Tuesday

_____

Wednesday

_____

Thursday

_____

Friday

_____

Saturday

_____

Sunday

_____

Priorities

To Do

★

★

★

★

Notes

My Training Week

Coach Name: _____

Hours Trained: _____

Achievements: _____

How I felt ☹ 😕 😐 🙂 😃

Conditioning notes

Skill:	Rep:

Coach Said:

Best thing this week:

I am grateful for

Week ----------

You only see obstacles when you take your eye off the goal.

Monday
_____

Tuesday
_____

Wednesday
_____

Thursday
_____

Friday
_____

Saturday
_____

Sunday
_____

Priorities

To Do
* ★
* ★
* ★
* ★

Notes

My Training Week

Coach Name: _____

Hours Trained: _____

Achievements: _____

How I felt   ☹ 😕 😐 🙂 😄

Conditioning notes

Skill:	Rep:

Coach Said:

Best thing this Week:

*I am
grateful for*

Week ....

Let your mistakes make you better not bitter.

Monday
_____

Tuesday
_____

Wednesday
_____

Thursday
_____

Friday
_____

Saturday
_____

Sunday
_____

Priorities

To Do
- ★
- ★
- ★
- ★

Notes

My Training Week

Coach Name: _____

Hours Trained: _____

Achievements: _____

How I felt ☹ 🙁 😐 🙂 😃

Conditioning notes

Skill:	Rep:

Coach Said:

Best thing this week:

I am
grateful for

Week ....

Practice like you've never Won.
Play like you've never Lost.

Monday

_____

Tuesday

_____

Wednesday

_____

Thursday

_____

Friday

_____

Saturday

_____

Sunday

_____

Priorities

To Do

★

★

★

★

Notes

My Training Week

Coach Name: _____

Hours Trained: _____

Achievements: _____

How I felt   ☹ 😐 😐 🙂 😃

Conditioning notes

Skill:	Rep:

Coach Said: Best thing this week:

I am grateful for

Week ◆◆◆◆◆◆◆◆

Hard work makes things look easy.

Monday

_____

Tuesday

_____

Wednesday

_____

Thursday

_____

Friday

_____

Saturday

_____

Sunday

_____

Priorities

To Do

★

★

★

★

Notes

My Training Week

Coach Name: _____

Hours Trained: _____

Achievements: _____

How I felt   ☹ 😐 😐 🙂 😃

Conditioning notes

Skill:	Rep:

Coach Said:

Best thing this week:

I am grateful for

Week ••••••••

Sometimes you win, sometimes you learn.

Monday

_____

Tuesday

_____

Wednesday

_____

Thursday

_____

Friday

_____

Saturday

_____

Sunday

_____

Priorities

To Do

★

★

★

★

Notes

My Training Week

Coach Name: _____

Hours Trained: _____

Achievements: _____

How I felt ☹ 🙂 😐 🙂 😃

Conditioning notes

Skill:	Rep:

Coach Said:

Best thing this Week:

I am grateful for

Week ....

Be so good that they can't ignore you.

Monday

_____

Tuesday

_____

Wednesday

_____

Thursday

_____

Friday

_____

Saturday

_____

Sunday

_____

Priorities

To Do

- ★
- ★
- ★
- ★

Notes

My Training Week

Coach Name: _____

Hours Trained: _____

Achievements: _____

How I felt 😞 🙂 😐 🙂 😄

Conditioning notes

Skill:	Rep:

Coach Said:

Best thing this Week:

I am grateful for

Week •••••••••

When you are giving up,
someone else is still going.

Monday
_____

Tuesday
_____

Wednesday
_____

Thursday
_____

Friday
_____

Saturday
_____

Sunday
_____

Priorities

To Do
★
★
★
★

Notes

My Training Week

Coach Name: _____

Hours Trained: _____

Achievements: _____

How I felt   ☹ 🙂 😐 🙂 😃

Conditioning notes

Skill:	Rep:

Coach Said:

Best thing this Week:

I am
grateful for

Week •••••••••

Don't let anyone ever dull your sparkle.

Monday

_____

Tuesday

_____

Wednesday

_____

Thursday

_____

Friday

_____

Saturday

_____

Sunday

_____

Priorities

To Do

★

★

★

★

Notes

My Training Week

Coach Name: _____

Hours Trained: _____

Achievements: _____

How I felt ☹ ☹ ☺ ☺ ☺

Conditioning notes

Skill:	Rep:

Coach Said:

Best thing this Week:

I am grateful for

Week ●●●●●●●●●

Everything you want is on the other side of fear.

Monday
_____

Tuesday
_____

Wednesday
_____

Thursday
_____

Friday
_____

Saturday
_____

Sunday
_____

Priorities

To Do
* ★
* ★
* ★
* ★

Notes

My Training Week

Coach Name: _____

Hours Trained: _____

Achievements: _____

How I felt ☹ 🙂 😐 🙂 😃

Conditioning notes

Skill:	Rep:

Coach Said:

Best thing this week:

I am grateful for

Week •◆•◆•◆•◆•◆◆

You don't have to see the whole staircase to take the first step.

Monday

_____

Tuesday

_____

Wednesday

_____

Thursday

_____

Friday

_____

Saturday

_____

Sunday

_____

Priorities

To Do

- ★
- ★
- ★
- ★

Notes

My Training Week

Coach Name: _____

Hours Trained: _____

Achievements: _____

How I felt ☹ 🙂 😐 🙂 😃

Conditioning notes

Skill:	Rep:

Coach Said:

Best thing this week:

I am grateful for

Be a light to the world.

Week ●◆●◆●◆●◆●◆●

Monday

_____

Tuesday

_____

Wednesday

_____

Thursday

_____

Friday

_____

Saturday

_____

Sunday

_____

Priorities

To Do

- ★
- ★
- ★
- ★

Notes

My Training Week

Coach Name: _____

Hours Trained: _____

Achievements: _____

How I felt ☹ 😐 😐 🙂 😀

Conditioning notes

Skill:	Rep:

Coach Said:

Best thing this week:

I am
grateful for

Week ....

There is always room to improve. Always.

Monday
_____

Tuesday
_____

Wednesday
_____

Thursday
_____

Friday
_____

Saturday
_____

Sunday
_____

Priorities

To Do

- ★
- ★
- ★
- ★

Notes

My Training Week

Coach Name: _____

Hours Trained: _____

Achievements: _____

How I felt ☹ 🙂 😐 🙂 😃

Conditioning notes

Skill:	Rep:

Coach Said:

Best thing this week:

I am grateful for

Week ....

The pain you feel today is the strength you feel tomorrow.

Monday

_____

Tuesday

_____

Wednesday

_____

Thursday

_____

Friday

_____

Saturday

_____

Sunday

_____

Priorities

To Do

- ★
- ★
- ★
- ★

Notes

My Training Week

Coach Name: _____

Hours Trained: _____

Achievements: _____

How I felt ☹ 😕 😐 🙂 😀

Conditioning notes

Skill:	Rep:

Coach Said:

Best thing this week:

I am grateful for

You only fail when you stop trying.

Week ◆◆◆◆◆◆◆◆

Monday

_____

Tuesday

_____

Wednesday

_____

Thursday

_____

Friday

_____

Saturday

_____

Sunday

_____

Priorities

To Do

★

★

★

★

Notes

My Training Week

Coach Name: _____

Hours Trained: _____

Achievements: _____

How I felt ☹ 🙂 😐 🙂 😃

Conditioning notes

Skill:	Rep:

Coach Said:

Best thing this Week:

I am grateful for

Week ....

Without risk there is no reward.

Monday

_____

Tuesday

_____

Wednesday

_____

Thursday

_____

Friday

_____

Saturday

_____

Sunday

_____

Priorities

To Do

- ★
- ★
- ★
- ★

Notes

My Training Week

Coach Name: _____

Hours Trained: _____

Achievements: _____

How I felt   ☹ 🙂 😐 🙂 😄

Conditioning notes

Skill:	Rep:

Coach Said:

Best thing this week:

I am grateful for

Don't Quit

by

John Greenleaf Whittier

When things go wrong as they sometimes will,

When the road you're walking seems all up hill,

When the money is low and the debts are high

And you want to smile, but you have to sigh,

When life is getting you down a bit,

Rest if you must, but don't you quit!

Life is strange with its twists and turns

As every one of us sometimes learns

And many a failure comes about

When we might have won had we stuck it out;

Don't give up though the pace seems slow—

You may succeed with another blow.

Success is failure turned inside out—

The silver tint of the clouds of doubt,

And you never can tell just how close you are,

It may be near when it seems so far;

So stick to the fight when you're hardest hit—

It's when things seem worst that you....

MUST NOT QUIT

 # My Meets

Meet: _____

Level: _____

Vault   Score [   ]   Place [   ]

How I felt   ☹ ☺ 😐 🙂 😄

Bars   Score [   ]   Place [   ]

How I felt   ☹ ☺ 😐 🙂 😄

Beam   Score [   ]   Place [   ]

How I felt   ☹ ☺ 😐 🙂 😄

Floor   Score [   ]   Place [   ]

How I felt   ☹ ☺ 😐 🙂 😄

Notes _____
_____
_____

My Meets

Meet: _____

Level: _____

Vault   Score [   ]   Place [   ]

How I felt   😞 😊 😐 🙂 😃

Bars   Score [   ]   Place [   ]

How I felt   😞 😊 😐 🙂 😃

Beam   Score [   ]   Place [   ]

How I felt   😞 😊 😐 🙂 😃

Floor   Score [   ]   Place [   ]

How I felt   😞 😊 😐 🙂 😃

Notes _____

_____

_____

My Meets

Meet: _____

Level: _____

Vault   Score [   ]   Place [   ]

How I felt ☹ 😐 😐 🙂 😄

Bars   Score [   ]   Place [   ]

How I felt ☹ 😐 😐 🙂 😄

Beam   Score [   ]   Place [   ]

How I felt ☹ 😐 😐 🙂 😄

Floor   Score [   ]   Place [   ]

How I felt ☹ 😐 😐 🙂 😄

Notes _____
_____
_____

My Meets

Meet: _____

Level: _____

<u>Vault</u>   Score [   ]   Place [   ]

How I felt   ☹ 🙂 😐 🙂 😃

<u>Bars</u>   Score [   ]   Place [   ]

How I felt   ☹ 🙂 😐 🙂 😃

<u>Beam</u>   Score [   ]   Place [   ]

How I felt   ☹ 🙂 😐 🙂 😃

<u>Floor</u>   Score [   ]   Place [   ]

How I felt   ☹ 🙂 😐 🙂 😃

Notes _____
_____
_____

 # My Meets

Meet: _____

Level: _____

Vault   Score [ ]   Place [ ]

How I felt ☹ 😕 😐 🙂 😄

Bars   Score [ ]   Place [ ]

How I felt ☹ 😕 😐 🙂 😄

Beam   Score [ ]   Place [ ]

How I felt ☹ 😕 😐 🙂 😄

Floor   Score [ ]   Place [ ]

How I felt ☹ 😕 😐 🙂 😄

Notes _____
_____
_____

My Meets

Meet: _____

Level: _____

<u>Vault</u>   Score [ ]   Place [ ]

How I felt   😦 🙂 😐 ☺ 😃

<u>Bars</u>   Score [ ]   Place [ ]

How I felt   😦 🙂 😐 ☺ 😃

<u>Beam</u>   Score [ ]   Place [ ]

How I felt   😦 🙂 😐 ☺ 😃

<u>Floor</u>   Score [ ]   Place [ ]

How I felt   😦 🙂 😐 ☺ 😃

Notes _____
_____
_____

My Meets

Meet: _____

Level: _____

Vault
Score [   ]   Place [   ]

How I felt 😞 😌 😐 🙂 😁

Bars
Score [   ]   Place [   ]

How I felt 😞 😌 😐 🙂 😁

Beam
Score [   ]   Place [   ]

How I felt 😞 😌 😐 🙂 😁

Floor
Score [   ]   Place [   ]

How I felt 😞 😌 😐 🙂 😁

Notes _____

_____

_____

My Meets

Meet: _____

Level: _____

Vault   Score [   ]   Place [   ]

How I felt ☹ 🙁 😐 🙂 😃

Bars   Score [   ]   Place [   ]

How I felt ☹ 🙁 😐 🙂 😃

Beam   Score [   ]   Place [   ]

How I felt ☹ 🙁 😐 🙂 😃

Floor   Score [   ]   Place [   ]

How I felt ☹ 🙁 😐 🙂 😃

Notes _____
_____
_____

My Meets

Meet: _____

Level: _____

___

Vault   Score [   ]   Place [   ]

How I felt   ☹ 😕 😐 🙂 😃

___

Bars   Score [   ]   Place [   ]

How I felt   ☹ 😕 😐 🙂 😃

___

Beam   Score [   ]   Place [   ]

How I felt   ☹ 😕 😐 🙂 😃

___

Floor   Score [   ]   Place [   ]

How I felt   ☹ 😕 😐 🙂 😃

___

Notes _____

_____

_____

 # My Meets

Meet: _____

Level: _____

Vault Score [ ] Place [ ]

How I felt ☹ 🙁 😐 🙂 😃

Bars Score [ ] Place [ ]

How I felt ☹ 🙁 😐 🙂 😃

Beam Score [ ] Place [ ]

How I felt ☹ 🙁 😐 🙂 😃

Floor Score [ ] Place [ ]

How I felt ☹ 🙁 😐 🙂 😃

Notes _____
_____
_____

 # My Meets

Meet: _____

Level: _____

Vault   Score [ ]   Place [ ]

How I felt   😦 🙂 😐 🙂 😄

Bars   Score [ ]   Place [ ]

How I felt   😦 🙂 😐 🙂 😄

Beam   Score [ ]   Place [ ]

How I felt   😦 🙂 😐 🙂 😄

Floor   Score [ ]   Place [ ]

How I felt   😦 🙂 😐 🙂 😄

Notes _____

_____

_____

We dance for laughter
We dance for tears
We dance for madness
We dance for fears
We dance for hopes
We dance for screams
We are the dancers
We create the dreams

−   Albert Einstein

Word Search

```
Q G J I W Z H E G V N X G T U C K
A R H Y T H M I C A T Y I A I X H
G T R A I N I N G U P Y A W W X X
G R I P S S E V P L L R N S H R N
S I B U T X D Y G T D X T B A R S
K P Z C R R C A R T W H E E L X B
I S H P A L H H A N D S T A N D Y
L R U Z D P A X F I K N B G Q G A
L Z U Q D I N T C C I X L T Z Y C
M T U C L K D T H L P T E A M M R
T B M U E E S Z A M O U N T F N O
F L O O R Q P C L F P V P H V A B
Y A G E A Y R R K B E A M S H S A
B U I G J H I B L E O T A R D T T
W S A L T O N B A F G D R T C C I
I H L E G P G A R T I S T I C Q C
Z O L Y M P I C S D U J W Y H D S
```

HANDSPRING, HANDSTAND, CHALK,
CARTWHEEL, TEAM, RHYTHMIC, LEOTARD,
GIANT, RIPS, ACROBATICS, FLOOR, STRADDLE,
VAULT, SALTO, MOUNT, KIP, OLYMPICS,
TRAINING, TUCK, PIKE, GYMNAST, ARTISTIC,
BEAM, GRIPS, BARS, SKILL

Notes

Notes

Notes

Notes

Notes

Made in United States
Orlando, FL
27 November 2021

10829168R00079